Soulless Baggage

By

Tori Richey

Soulless Baggage

By Tori Richey

Preface

Oliver Wendell Holmes once said that "I think that, life is action and passion, it is required of man that he should share the passion and action of his time as peril of being judged not to have lived." There were trials and tribulations that I have endured over the years of being born into this famine, and diseased infested world. Many events has led to my rise from the ashes of which I came. Whether it be discovering my homosexuality, peer pressure, alcoholic father, child abuse, rape, or even teaching the children who has no one to turn too. All of these things have made me what what I am. They are who I am and was.

I never really knew who I was in life, until I was in kindergarten. There was this boy name Jason. He was so adorable. The jacket he wore, yellow and blue, and to this day, yellow and blue are my favorite colors. Jason would hang out with me when it was break time, and he would put his hand on my shoulders, and I would just melt. My brother was always by my side, he was two years older than I was. There was this castle in the middle of the play ground. A stone barrier to all that oppressed us. We would go in the castle and kiss. I knew who I was at a young age, but I never knew what I was. I was caught up on the cycle of being loved and being free.

Soulless Baggage

By Tori Richey

We were caught by the nuns that rans the facility. After Jason and I kissed, that was the last time I saw him. He never returned to the castle that made me a prince before time.

Elementary school, were hottie central. I saw so many boys, that I was so attracted to. Jon my little Asian friend; was so cute that I could just pick him up and hold him in my arms. He was so small, and so fragile, that I wanted to protect him from any one that would do him harm. Jon hung out with another boy, name john, and I was heartbroken. I never really had a chance. I was overweight, I felt unattractive, and I was a know it all in school. When Valentines Day came, I received paper hearts from girls, but never found my true Valentine. It is the loneliness that makes the loudness of noise.

I came to realize, love is not for me. I see it all the time. Especially in my own home. My mother were so innocent and so naive that she would stay in a marriage that was not a marriage at all. She wanted to endure the alcoholic rage from my father. God bless his soul, he is not deceased yet, however, his soul died when he made our life a living hell. He would rant and rage, and strike my mother. My mother was not the person to stand by to allow any abuse. My father came in one day from his alcohol binge, and struck my mother while she was ironing his his uniform for work. She looked at him with a tear running down her face, and took the iron, and smashed it against his face.

Soulless Baggage — By Tori Richey

While my father was down, she went around to him, and took the hot end of the iron, and place it on his face. She told him, in a tone that I have never heard before, "I want you to remember this day. Whenever you look in the mirror, you will know, to never place a hand on me again." After that, he never did. However, that was not my mothers last time. My mother hit him with the skillet, while she was cooking spaghetti and meatballs.
I never cried, because that was the norm for my household. My father, started staying out later, and later, every night. I started to blame myself, that maybe I could have done something. If I could, then maybe my father would be here.

Being gay was not easy to hide. My mother use to give me dolls and stuffed animals to play with. And I use to comb their hair, and make sure they are were pretty for the ball. I use to imagine that they were someone I could turn to, and have when ever my parents would have their little prized fight bouts. My mother is still the undisputed champion to this day.

Gender bending was a quite episode for me. I use to try on my mothers blouses and bras. I looked so pretty, that I slid on her shoes with the back out. They were gold hi-heels with a red trim around them. My father came in one day, while I was modeling in front of the mirror. He slapped me across the face, and it left a big blue bruise.

Soulless Baggage
By Tori Richey

I am a black male, and it left a bruise, I was shocked. I didn't know that was possible. After he ripped my mothers clothes off of me, I lay there naked, and embarrassed. I wanted to die that moment.

My father looked at me with those red intense eyes, and said, "well since you looked like a women I am going to treat you like a women."So my father raped me that day. After that, I was in the shower, and tried to get his drool off of me, and his foul smelling breath out of my mind. After that session, he never really looked at me the same, and I have never looked at him the same either.

I never told my mother what happened. I never told anyone, because if my mother knew, she would have killed him.

I knew that my mother would be convicted of his murder, and be taken away from me. Now my mother was not a gem herself. She would call me names, but she would never assault me like my father did.

High school was nothing like Elementary school. There were different groups, clicks as you would called them. I wanted to fit in. I wanted to have friends. I was very stocky, and some people picked on me. I never said anything. I would walk up the street and catch the bus to go to school. While on the bus, they use to tease me. I was the first one on the bus, and the last one off. I was timid boy.

Soulless Baggage

By Tori Richey

One day while just minding my business. I was looking out of the window, and watching life pass me by, I and I was looking at homes, and houses, and wondering, why couldn't I be born white? Why did I become a black martyr at a young age?" This boy named Jamar, teased me, and he slapped me. That slap woke up a demon in me. I was all over him. I punched him in the nose, and mouth, and was kicking him in the head. I almost killed him. People pulled me off of him, and I was removed from the bus after that incident. I am my mother's son. I was never picked on again after that. However, many other kids were picked on and humiliated. There was this boy name Mark. He wore glasses, kind of stocky, and was in a wheelchair. His tormentor was a boy name Alfred. He would push him around and call him names. Hurtful names. I intervened and punch Alfred in the face, and I was sent to the Deans office.
I told the dean what happened, and so did Mark, and the dean excused me.

That was a moment I decided to defend the ones that could not defend themselves. I use to pick on the bullies. I bullied the bully sorta speak. At this time, no one knew I was gay. I was hiding it very well. There were so many boys I wanted to have, and to kiss, and to hold, but I would not dare to ask on a date. Except a boy name Jason. He was like the Jason I had kissed in kindergarten. He was so sweet, and was not a fighter.

Soulless Baggage

By Tori Richey

I defended him against a rollie pollie boy name Charlie. No one wanted to go against me. Jason and I dated, and I found out he had a girlfriend on the side, and I never talked to him again. I went out for foot ball. I never really like the game. I just wanted to hurt people. I was on the team for a year. I was the defense tackle. When people came at me, I would put them down, and most of the time, they stayed down.

I would use moves, like clotheslines, and neck breakers. I was suspended, and then thrown off the team. I still had a need to fit in. I wanted people to love me, not fear me. So I tried the next best thing. I went out for cheer-leading. I wanted those red and white pom poms. I wanted to root for my boys. I started to do cartwheels, and cheer, and every body started to come out from nowhere to see me. I guess the secret is out now. I am a queer. The day after the tryouts, the ones that made it, their names were on the list. I scoured that page, up and down, side to side, and nowhere was my name on it.

I was devastated. I decided I do not need to fit in, I just need to make my mother proud. So I started to study computers, and anything that interested me. I went to other schools, taking up courses, and really challenging myself.

I met a boy name Michael, and he took my world by storm. He would tickle me, and held my hand when no one was looking he kissed me.

Soulless Baggage   By Tori Richey

I wanted him to be mines forever. We wanted to got to the prom together, but same-sex couples were not allowed. So I went back to gender bending. I walked in to the prom with a blue sequence gown, and a shall on my shoulders. I managed to dance in blue high heels. That night was amazing. Dancing under the beautiful streamers, and listening to Luther Vandross, "If the world was mine," I was in heaven.

Michael and I hit it off well. I went to school in Arizona, for school for two years and came back to good ole Las Vegas. Michael waited for me. Michael had changed. He was into crack cocaine. He had me try it. Its was a sensation that I never felt. I felt all things did not matter as long as I was high. God did not even matter to me. I felt so selfish, that I wanted more and more. And I knew I was addicted. Michael and I were so close, that no one mattered to us, not even my mother. Things came to an end when Michael went to prison. I was alone, and addicted to crack cocaine. I started to drink alcohol, and driving drunk. Life was not meant for me. I was trying everything to have the breath in my lungs taken from my soul. Death is the golden key to an eternity without pain or suffering.

I wanted to die, but the grave is a private, and peaceful place, but no one seems to embrace it. I was fearful of dying.

Soulless Baggage

By Tori Richey

I was like a runaway child who refused to go home, but was afraid to stay on the streets.

I am still battling demons from my day as a junkie. I am still counting the days I am clean. I do not want to smell the stench of failure that looms from the pipe that I use to smoke. My brother has a little daughter. Her name is Isis, and she really loves me. And I really love her. Not too many people know that I did father a child when I was in high school. His name was Jason Alexander. His mother was Vivian. That name for a beautiful girl, did her justice. She was something. Vivian, would look like an Egyptian queen. She would look at me with eyes that screamed for understanding. We had sex, only once, and after that one time. I look into her eyes, and I told her, "I'm gay." She freaked out, and told me she did not want to see me again. Four months later, she told me she was pregnant, and I was the father. I was ecstatic.

My son was born into this world, by a gay man. Vivian did not want me to see him, nor touch him. I saw my son the day I was set to move to Arizona. I graduated from high school, and Vivian called me, and told me to come by to see my son before I leave for Arizona. I jumped into my little Chevy Impala, and headed over to her house. I rang the door bell, and I saw Vivian, and she looked so radiant, and she handed me my son.

Soulless Baggage

By Tori Richey

He was so beautiful, and so unreal, because I never knew what I felt to have a life that I created in my arms.

I kissed his forehead, and hours just flew by. I had to leave, and go to school, and I was so distraught to leave my son again.

I arrived in Arizona, and it was like heaven. It was hot as hell, but the people had great attitudes. Vivian wanted to surprise me. She was coming over to see me with Jason by her side, all bundled up in his car seat, with his stuffed Winnie the pooh bear in his lap. Vivian made a wrong turn, and went off the side of the mountain. They died on impact.

The car was upside down, and was like someone placed it in those machines that crushes cars at the junk yard. I went insane when I heard the news, and my boyfriend at the time, timothy, was by my side, and he never left. I wanted to die, my friends took turns on a suicide watch, and I am very grateful they did, or would not be telling you this story right now.

I found a new love here in Las Vegas. I moved back after I graduated and received a degree in graphic arts. I never used the degree. I vowed never to draw again Vivian and Jason gave up their life because I wanted to draw for a living. The price of being an artist, were two lives.

Soulless Baggage   By Tori Richey

William Hazlitt once said "Rules and Models, destroy genus and art," Art is a passing trend to me. My past has created this being before you. I know God has a plan. But why does a perfect plan, from a perfect being, have so much depression and chaos? It does not matter. I am who I am and I am releasing this baggage. Upon you.

Sincerely
Tori Richey

Now Entering Soulless Baggage

Soulless Baggage By Tori Richey

Coming To Grips

It was you that helped me see that life was not heaven, but a way to enter into the heavenly gates with a story to tell. So many things I have done that shed frowns on many faces. So many people who will not bother to come to my final passing.

It's okay. I have you. No one wants to close their eyes, and wake up with dirt on their eyelids. I'm going to see my mother. She will not recognize me. I'm an old woman, who has been beaten, abused and robbed of materialistic things, and the other was my heart.

My precious children, waited until one foot was in the grave, before they took my hard earned money. But I have you. I see your eyes filling with water, and I saw your lip tremble.

When I go, do not hold on, and I promise I will let go when he comes to take me away. My mother will not recognize me, but she will know who I am.

I am going to close my eyes now. Just for a little bit of rest. If you do not see my pretty brown eyes in the morning, you know me and my mother are talking about old times.

Do not cry. Do not let your lip quiver.
Life is not the end, because death is the beginning.

That Time

I danced with you, and I walked many roads less traveled, Until that night. You were different. You were not the man I fell in love with. The one that assisted me in beating down the demons and the ghouls that tried to hurt what we took minutes, hours and seconds to create.

That night, I saw red in your eyes as you beat down the woman that gave birth to you. Fucking lies. It was all fucking lies. You were apart of the that crew. The devils sons. The pricks that took their aggression out on the weak individuals.

I could not let you walk that road alone. I had to take away the pain that you provoked, invoked and really wasn't that what you wanted? To take the pain away? I took the firing tool to lay many bullets into you. Like pac man, the power pellets turned you into a ghost. Like pac man, I withered once you died. I cried over your dead and motionless body. I cried until my heart grew cold. That night.

I know its in the past. I know its all gone. I know its what I had to do. I know I will face judgment in the end. But it was you that judged me. Judged me not to stop you from hurting me. You was wrong, like me. I was wrong to hold you until the sun came up and dance until we grew weary. Eyes closing. No emotion. I am sorry for the death. For I died too. Like you. That night.

Soulless Baggage   By Tori Richey

Mouth

It's your smile. The taste of your body, the ending and
the beginning of your skin. So intact so eloquent.

I fear the unknown, because I know
the unknown.

I want to speak to you. To yell. To raise a fuss. I
remain quiet, tucked into a little shell, so I wont fall
apart.

No love exist, in this world for a lonely man.
No love exist, in the my heart for any man.
I hear the false trebles that aligns your throat.
I hear the bullshit that comes out of the hole
that is called your mouth.

This device was meant for eating, not for spouting
lies.

I don't know you. However I do know why you were
sent to me. To test me. To make me insane. To
become the fighter I once was.

I will become the soulless individual that
people see but never recognize. I will be
the soulless man that I will see when I look into
the mirror. Cold I once was. Cold is what I will
become. Again,

Soulless Baggage By Tori Richey

Daddy's Little Girl

Did you look at me when you struck me with your
iron fist? You saw my tears and you saw my
bleeding wrist. I wanted it to stop. I wanted
peace for a chance. Then you made me kiss you
on your cheek, and open your filthy pants.
I will always be your little girl. That is what I was
born to be. I lay still, staring at the picture of my
mother. Wishing she would have chosen some else as
her lover. Wishing she would have chosen another.

Someone that loved her until death do they apart. Not
only did you take her last breath, but you broke her
heart. I was the only one left to kiss and touch. I will
always be your little girl. Isn't that what you told me?
Now I remember who I was meant to be. A mature
lady, and responsible citizen. Walking to church,
praying to our Lord, and confessing my sins.

As I sit here, behinds these bars, tears running
down my face. I feel a weight have been lifted off my
crumbling shoulders. It's freedom I taste.

No matter how many times I wash my hands. I will
always see the blood from that filthy filthy man. I
will always be your little girl any way. But daddy,
your little girl grew up that day. The day you went
away. Good bye daddy. Hello Life.

Soulless Baggage By Tori Richey

Landing In Las Vegas

I woke up today in Las Vegas, As the devil was touching me. And all I could think about was someday, Maybe someday you will come around.

If this loneliness preys on me much longer,
I don't know what I would do. You got to understand it's a hard knock life, that I'm going through.

And when the darkness falls around me, and I don't think I'll make it through. I need your love to guide me, the only person I want to be with is you.

My mama is getting kinda crazy, and my dad is getting kind of old. I keep my head from getting hazy, I just can't wait until you come home.

And all these lonely days, I am not okay, I'll make up for my sins, this I swear. I need your love to hold me up, when it's too much, I shed a tear.

And when the darkness falls around me, and I don't think I'll make it through. I need your love to guide me, the only person I want to be with is you.

And all these lonely days, I am not okay.
I'll make up for my sins, this I swear.
I need your love to hold me up,
when it's too much, I shed a tear.

Begin

Once it begins, there is no stopping it. The rage is so intense that the means outweighs the justification. I saw it looming in the air, and to no avail, I was helpless in guiding its spirit to overtake its superiority.

I saw your eyes. I saw the anxiety reached its limits and the pupils succumbed the entire eye socket. I wished I was you. To be on the other end of my own rage to see how powerful I truly am.

I will never wither away. I will never achieve the maximum of happiness and the sickening thud of a joyful silence. Accepted the fate of a dying mankind. I accepted the fate of a fallen man. I have accepted the fate of this falling man.

Once it begins, there is no stopping it. My rage is so intense that the means outweighs the justification. It loomed in the air, and to no avail, I was not able to control it. Nor did I wanted to. You were helpless when I inflicted my rage on you. And for that, you are truly sorry.

Soulless Baggage By Tori Richey

Bestow

Another day young child. You have seen a lot, and there is more to see. But let me tell you what I saw when I saw you then. I saw my child, standing tall through the thick and thin.

I saw my child, growing strong in weary world. But never let the clouds of despair settle in. I saw my child defending herself, and defending others to the best of her ability, and to say I am ready to be put to the test.

I saw a woman that went through the pain of labor and stood tall after the birth with a smile that can shed the frowns of the meanest man that ever woke up in crowded and less pleasant of a world.

Now I tell you what I see when I see you now. I see a woman who depends on others, to shed even a drop of gladness in her life. I see a woman who is so tired and wishes that it all disappear, if you just shut your eyes and count to ten.

I see a woman who not only have withered into the catacombs of a forgotten vessel, but remembers the past every minute of every day. She watches moving pictures and moving people that rally around her.

Soulless Baggage

By Tori Richey

My child, this was not meant to pick up your spirits, but more to set you back on the path that whence you came.

I will now tell you what I see when I look to your future. I see a woman who stands tall yet again. I see a smile on her face, not because she does not receive love, but because she know she is love.

Do not waste any precious moments while you are on earth. The ones that yells and complains to you, turn a deaf ear, and listen to my words when I speak.

I will see you soon. Not today. However, until that day, my child, I want to see you become the woman I have created, prepared, and has given as gift to the world that does not deserve such treasure.

Happy Birthday My child. For this is just the beginning and never will it end. Just so you know; I stop carrying you through the tough times, but I was always walking beside you, just in case you needed me. Never fall away, but if you do, my child, I will catch you. I will catch you. Every step of the way.

Soulless Baggage   By Tori Richey

Fail With Me In The Dark

Death and destruction is how we show our love.
Denial of forgiveness in our mind because
we blame it on each other desperately.
This is how Jesus died,
saving the blind and baptizing the ones with pride.
We blame it on each other independently.
We fail.
We're frail
Wearing a veil.
All in all
We fail.
Too much pride to cry for help.
Too busy killing ourselves.
We blame it on each other transcendentally
Maybe we are a different breed.
We are losers because we are not listening.
Blame it on the bottle. Respectfully.
We fail.
We're frail
Wearing a veil.
All in all
We fail.

Soulless Baggage   By Tori Richey

Martyr

I sit back gasping and was lured back into the fold. He told me so. He sold me bro. The lights went like out like Georgia, not a sound dared to make a peep. I took a step, more like a leap.

He crept into my soul, unable to have use of my arms or legs, he is in control. I fall away, breathing hard, nothing in his way, blocking my view, withering. Just withering. Nothing to show, but skin and bones.

The skin fall to ground. So slimy to the touch. I love my basking prince, love you so much. I don't know what to do if you leave my sight. Like a blind man I need you to guide me into the light. Never stay in darkness, for if I leave I am a marked man, understand?

It's not a song. Nor a poem. Nor a statement. Just judgment. What is your verdict my love. Guilty. He spoke in a hush tone, he lifted his arms above my head, and left me alone, to smile upside down.

No one around but me and my thoughts. I am caught up all in love, not even the angels are singing from above. I lost it. It's all gone. Leave me alone and let me walk to grave still hearing mama said baby behave, I was sentenced to death. Now what do you think of me. Mama am I still your baby?

Soulless Baggage — By Tori Richey

I Don't Need

I find you impossible.
I find you intolerable.
I find you inconsiderate of
my feelings and my insecurities.
Those things does not bother me.

The world is so uncomfortable with
my views and thoughts, that they would
turn their back and walk away into the night
without uttering a word of content of good intentions.

With all your faults, I can see through your piercing
armor. You may look down your nose at me, and wish
my orientation, that explicit, my sexuality is of a
rewarding one, but you want the best for me. I can
see it in your scorching blue eyes.

I may find you impossible.
I may find you Intolerable.
I may even find you inconsiderate of my
feelings and thoughts. Those things will
never bother me, because you will always
be my friend.

Soulless Baggage   By Tori Richey

End Of Days

There are children standing here. Eyes staring blindly at the cloudless sky. Dried blood caked on their face.

He has been here. Men lays in beds that becomes their graves. Fathers lost without a trace. A nation blind to their disgrace. Since he's been here.

And I see no bravery. No bravery in your eyes anymore. Only sadness.

Houses burnt beyond repair. The smell of death is in the air. A woman weeping in despair says, he has been here. Tracer lighting up the sky. It's another families' turn to die. A child afraid to even cry out says, he has been here.

And I see no bravery. No bravery in your eyes anymore. Only sadness.

There are children standing here. Arms outstretched into the sky. But no one asks the question. Will he ever come back? Old men kneel to accept their fate. Wives and daughters cut and raped. A generation drenched in hate. Since he left.

And I see no bravery. No bravery in your eyes anymore. Only sadness.

Soulless Baggage   By Tori Richey

Do you remember

Do you remember when we first talked? How you I trembled when you spoke to me. Do you remember how you touched my heart? How it shivered every time I got close to you.

I remember it all. From the days of when loneliness

enraged my self-hating soul. You were there to make me beautiful. Do you remember when we stopped talking? The day that all life didn't matter anymore.

Do you remember what you said to me? You told me that I mattered more than anyone you have ever known.

I remember it all. Wishing to take back what I said.

Wishing to hold you in my arms, If only if I could. There is nothing, more important than you.

Do you remember me holding your face in my callous hands, and telling you that you are more that what you see in the mirror? That your eyes were given to you by angels? I know you don't remember. Because I am telling you this now. You are an angel. That walks amongst us. Never forget that. My precious.

Fallen

I fell when you spoke my name. Fell like an misshapen boulder, gravitating to the earths surface. It was me you shattered into pieces and it was me, who swept up the debris.

Did I ever tell you that you meant the world to me? I did. I shouted to the heavens until my throat ran dry as the Las Vegas weather. To me, you were my God, my Jesus, my Lord, my way to find peace in an pathetic world that drifts to the wayside and aligns myself with self-doubt and lost self-esteem.

What was my wrongdoing in this relationship? My fall, my queer understanding of what love is suppose to be. I know who I am. I am the alpha and the omega of this vessel that is my body.

I pray for you, more than I pray for myself. I want to forgive you. I want to love you as I have loved you before.

It is you who I wait for. It is you who holds my heart and pulls my strings. I will wait until you walk back into my life, but do not keep me waiting. I am not patient to waste into nothing, but become something you refuse to give me.

Me.

Soulless Baggage   By Tori Richey

Reality

Reality. Is working against me.
Reality. Always keeping me down.

I'll never know what it is to be a man.
When everything goes to hell,
and I tried as hard as I can.
Doing the wrong things to throw
my happiness away.

Reality. Is working against me
Reality. always kept me down.

Doing right. Is not doing so good.
Blood stains. No one would
help me. Even if they could.
It's one more thing, that have
sent me to my knees.

Reality. Please don't come near me.
Reality. Has taken everyone from me
But how can that be?
Keep me alive. Just keep me alive

Soulless Baggage   By Tori Richey

My Funeral

Just as they lowered him into the ground. They dropped a rose onto the coffin and I heard a gasp. Fragments of his laughter looms us all. Riddle me this. A heart that is broken, still beats like a drum. He's in the ground.

You should have known the pain they inflicted on him. Tears felt like concrete. In every moment he swayed. Out of his mouth, the curses flew. Only the lonely, has to pay the price to live.

The house seems so empty. Damp from the collected tears on the pillow that you cried upon. One day this life will come to an end. Was he running from a monster, the one you created. The one who introduced him to his fate. A loomed dark figured who laid him to waste. He is in the ground.

You should have seen, the eyes turning red. Waiting for a hug, instead of the drugs instead. You saw the demons beside him, and you went away. In every moment he waited for you In every moment he sway.

Close your eyes, Say your grace.

Mark his name on his grave

Close your heart. Save your soul

Mark your name on your grave

Soulless Baggage By Tori Richey

Execution Date Not Set

I want to kiss the rose petals of your lips. They whisper so sweet with utter superiority. Lights out, and the party is over. It's so dark in here. Feeling trapped and inferior to your shadows. Just an image of a little boy looking out of the window, an seeing nothing, but rain. I want to run outside to feel every drop on my nose, but is afraid to get wet. The darkness is edging closer to me. I'm like a innocent man sentenced to death.

Did I do something wrong? What made you leave this world, without taking me by the hand into the clouds? To leave me here all alone. The opposite of a thief. You didn't just take my sex, my money, my self-esteem, but you took yourself from my sight. I didn't know, my Lord, could be so mean. An ordeal that drove this man to tears. Were you sincere? You want to hurt me in the dark.

You cursed the ground that I walk upon. And all I want to do now is curse you in return. For leaving this condemned soul to wander the earth, all alone. In the dark. It's like being on death row.

I don't understand why you had to go. I don't understand why you wish to hurt me in the dark. So leave me here. And let the darkness consume me. Until it is forever darkness. So dark. I am on death row. Awaiting my execution.

Soulless Baggage — By Tori Richey

One Turn

As you turn to me, you whispered sweet nothings into my ear. That is what they are called sweet nothings. You did not mean a word, nor did you

feel any remorse for what you did. You took it from me. I want it back. You touched me in places that was not meant for you. You went the extra mile to silence me and condemn me in this vessel which is my body.

I loathe you, and in turn I love you. I have to love you. I see you in the mirror when I put on my make up. I smell you whenever i drift off to sleep. I think about you when I am working my 9 to 5 job. I have to love you. You made me love you. I want a divorce from this nightmare.

We are through. I am through being this ragged doll who caresses her pillow, in thinking

that Jesus could save me from all that you have done. He gave me the strength, but it is me that will take my life back. I am the tin woman who keeps her heart from being raped and broken and thrown into the

Soulless Baggage

By Tori Richey

trash. I am that woman. I am the heartless woman you will see again. This time I will make sure you lay down, and stay down. Revenge is not sweet, but it is necessary.

I know you. I seen you around. We live in close proximity of one another. Mother would hate me if I told her what you did. Then again, maybe she will hate you.

Do not worry, it will not hurt. Remember those words you told me. It is to laugh. Say you love me, one last time, then I will cry when you lay still. Forgive me mother, for I have sinned. Lord forgive me for what I am about to do. Tin woman, is

going to live again, without freedom.

Freedom Of Thought

[Verse 1]

My face is what the devil sees before he goes to sleep.

Food for thought, he is the one that created us. and angels does not make a peep.

My father's dead, well he killed himself inside of me.

When he was inside of me, the dark clouds engulfed my identity.

I cut my wrist to see if I would bleed red.

Somebody call the pastor, this bastard is dying, or is the bastard already dead.

This meeting just begun, nigga I'm Satan's son.

I know I will not go to heaven. I am far from being the chosen one.

[Verse 2]

My mother raised me a single parent in a marriage with blood shed

I love my mother, if wasn't for her, I would be dead.

Lying in an unmarked grave no flowers or remains.

My mother does not have any money, but if I died, she would suffer internal pain.

I'm Odd. I'm not fucked up. Just mental

Crooked way, and crooked teeth. I need dental.

Soulless Baggage

By Tori Richey

[Verse 3]

I'm short, light skinned, my stomach is big as fuck.

I have to pay guys to sleep with me, the only way I can see a dick, in living color

I walk around without strain, no one to plead my case.

People say I am bubbly, but that be the other face.

Soak up the emotion and bleed it out like a tampon.

When I walk into a house, dim the lights, can not bare to have the lamp on.

This world is packed with too much evil to bare.

I am here waiting for my number to be called, it

can be heaven or hell, I really don't care.

[Verse 4]

I go from A to Z inside a fucking hour. Nothing to do.

Speaking and texting people, wondering why did we meet? Why did I have to meet you?

I stay clear minded, and never think about the past.

It was the past, that kicked this niggas black ass.

Yes to drugs, I been clean for only one fucking year.

By those means, you shouldn't look down your nose at me, you should cheer.

Soulless Baggage   By Tori Richey

[Verse 5]

My friends treat me like my father like a fucking stranger.

Wanting to cut them up, put them into OJ's white Ranger.

Oh yeah it was Bronco, lost my train of thought in a crowd.

All because I went to homecoming in a dress, no gays were allowed.

Every cell in my brain is encompassed by evil thoughts.

I'm the dream catcher but it nothing but nightmares I ever caught.

[Verse 6]

I don't wear green, because I don't have green in my pockets.

Fuck the monster in the closet, if hell is a virus we all caught it.

The doctor places his hand on my hand and told me it will be okay.

Wanting to get high on his medication and then isolate me and put me away.

I listen to Pink Floyd and it takes me on a trip.

I been told I am over stepping my bounds, but they aint going to do nothing, they aint going to do shit.

You're a sinner to. You can replay this conversation in church. I do.

Soulless Baggage

By Tori Richey

[Verse 7]

I graduated from college, but is still broke today.

My brother killed himself, he blew himself away.

I still remember the smell of his dead body, as it lay

emotionless, unconsciousness, and lifeless. But now he is okay.

I wanted my brother, I told my mother, she just looked at me with sad eyes.

It should have been me to die, no more worries no more cries.

Don't tell me you are sorry, don't even fucking bother

People came to my mother hugged her, for me, I got nada.

My imaginations and hallucinations are creations of bad situation.

Wanting to drop bombs like those thrill seekers in Boston out of desperation.

[Verse 8]

I know you hear me. and you want to ignore me.

But times I'm so serious you think I'm insane with a capital crazy.

Never to be a fresh prince of Bel Aire I imagine.

I am just a bad boy, Will Smith I am legend.

I roll with a false home and declaration of no independence.

Soulless Baggage

By Tori Richey

I created my own paradise, when I die, he will not let me in it.

Becoming a 40 year old rapper, talking about his past.

As I stated in Verse 4, the past is what kicked this niggas ass.

Impersonating to my peers, with the same problem for many years.

No way to solve them, but to go to a Father's Day convention with a bundle of tears.

Life's is what you make of it, not the other way around.

Take the cuts and the scrapes and never fall down.

My mother let us do what ever we want, just spoiled.

She never had that much when she was a girl, just a cotton and soil.

She wasn't careless, over protective like a bear.

Better looking than Bill Cosby's Clair.

My father didn't give a fuck, that is something he passed down to me.

My mom is all I have, if she dies, I will to, you will see.

When my so called family or friends decide to fucking share

This little fag boy, will get up walk out because I don't care.

Soulless Baggage

By Tori Richey

Life was not created to be heaven, but to be hell.

God created this world, and we are his property. We are prisoners in his jail.

[Verse 9]

My wrist is all red from the knife infliction's.

Dripping blood like water, I had good intentions.

You were never that equivalent to me Johnny, and I smile.

Well that's not his fucking name, but I think I fuck with you for a while.

Why do you want to know if I am stable, or am I in love?

Just because my bed is cold, just like my life and the angels above.

But I'm sitting here downing pills and just wishing an abrupt end.

With a tear they try to tell me its okay. But they just pretend.

Cause I shit and piss sitting down, never stand up for no one.

Maybe that is my problem, too consumed in thought of what my father has done.

Hopefully they see the boy that has not became a man.

I am a loser and never can win, finally, do you understand?

Soulless Baggage

By Tori Richey

My goal in life is to have someone to love me just for me and to hold me when I cry.

I'm suicidal, that is true. But soon we all are going to die.

This is my world. My circus. I hope you have heard me without fail.

I wish I had my best friends email, so I can tell him how much I fucking hate him in detail

Soulless Baggage   By Tori Richey

Those Ways

It's been so long. Being gay. They wish I would break down and say, Gods changed my ways. He change my ways. Those disgusting ways

I will never sell out. Don't get in my way. I will strike you down and make you pay. Until you change your ways. Matthew are you okay?

I wont hide. I have my pride. They will pay. for their evil ways. I found out. That hate grows cold. The God rose up, as I grow old. I cant change. No matter how much I pray. For their evil ways.

I wont hide. I have my pride. They will pay for what they did on that day. It's been so long, being gay. They kneel and pray and wish I would say Gods change my ways. He changed my ways. Those disgusting ways.

I will never sell out. Please don't get in my way. I will strike you down, and make you pay. Until you change your ways. Matthew are you sure you are okay?

Soulless Baggage — By Tori Richey

Midnight

It was you that held my hand when no one was there. It was you that helped me see that life was not heaven, but a way to enter into the heavenly gates with a story to tell.

So many things I have done that shed frowns on many faces. So many people who will not bother to come to my final passing. It's okay. I have you.

No one wants to close their eyes, and wake up with dirt on their eyelids. I'm going to see my mother. She will not recognize me. I'm an old woman, who has been beaten, abused and robbed of materialistic things, and the other was my heart. My precious children, waited until one foot was in the grave, before they took my hard earned money. But I have you.

I saw your eyes filling with water, and saw your lip tremble. When I go, do not hold on, and I promise I will let go when he comes to take me away. My mother will not recognize me, but she will know who I am. I am going to close my eyes now. Just for a little bit of rest. If you do not see my pretty brown eyes in the morning, you know me and my mother are talking about old times. Do not cry. Do not let your lip quiver. Life is not end, because death is the beginning.

Soulless Baggage — By Tori Richey

Again

It's your smile,
the taste of your body,
the ending and the beginning of
your skin. So intact so eloquent.
I fear the unknown, because I know
the unknown. I want to speak to you
to yell, to raise a fuss, I remain quiet
in a little shell so I wont fall apart.
No love in this world for a lonely man.
No love in the my heart for any man.
I hear the false trebles the aligns your throat.
I hear the bullshit that comes out of hole
the is called your mouth. This device was
meant for eating, not for spouting lies.
I don't know you. I don't know why you
were sent to me. To test me. To make me
insane. To become the fighter I once was.
I will become the soulless individual that
people see but never recognize. I will be
the soulless man that I see when I look into
the mirror. Cold I once was. Cold is what I will
become. Again.

Soulless Baggage   By Tori Richey

Underneath It All

Underneath it all,
they hate you.
They loathe you.
They decorate your grave
with black flowers.
They torment you.
They lie to you.
And in the end,
they are perceived as the
right ones. The godly ones.
And you are just dead.
Don't you see?
Wake up and smell
the fertilizer they are
raking over your grave.
Over your heart.
Don't you see?
They want you dead. Senator.
They want you dead.
I want you to run this country
better than anyone has ever dreamed.
But you ignore me. You sway like the
wind. And you pretend.
It all will come to past. I hope
it will not be your last.

www.ingramcontent.com/pod-product-compliance
Lightning Source LLC
Chambersburg PA
CBHW030031250526
45464CB00025B/1305